DISCOVERING YOUR HIDDEN POWER:

Unleashing the Power of Words

—∽—

By Julian Phillips
with Dr. A. R. Bernard

ACKNOWLEGEMENTS

—ɷ—

To GOD, "Me Roshema"!; my wife Barbara, the "Rock"; my parents Cecil & Enola, "Soul Survivors"; Cecile, Hollis, Holly, Emily, and Ashley, "God's Promise Secured"; Gary, the "Spark"; Pat, "God's Provider"; Thelma & Lloyd, "My Inspiration"; Frances, "Reverend Mother"; Hunter, Marlene, Kathy, Jaime and Hubert, "My Southern Comfort"; Carolyn, "My Heart"; Betty, Tony, Roger, JB, and Leroy "My Foundation"; Byron, "My Brother"; Luigi, "Mr. Consistent"; Charlie, "Mr. Generosity"; John, "The Banker"; Freddie, "Mr. Open Arms"; Henry, "The Duffer"; Rudy, "An Ever-Present Help"; Popsy, "The Gentle Giant"; Gerard, "Always Faithful"; Arnold, "My Willing Student"; my spiritual father Pastor A.R. Bernard, the "Visionary" and Elder Karen Bernard, my "Friend".

CONTENTS

—⚮—

INTRODUCTION

—w—

"Life is difficult…."

-M. Scott Peck-

I believe more than any other phrase written on paper, these three words perhaps best describe the existence for the majority of us who live on this planet called earth. Written by author and psychiatrist M. Scott Peck more than 25 years ago in his best seller, *"The Road Less Traveled"*, Peck attempts to reveal a fundamental truth—calling life what it is and not painting a rosy picture of it. Now I do not mean to suggest that life is all gloom and doom—not at all! There would be no hope at all—and it would be a terrible lie to even think we are living in some type of hell only to die at the end of this journey. However, for some of us, the day-to-day grind is a living hell and just making it to the end of the 24 hours is a miracle in and of itself. To a lesser degree for most of us, the word difficult means trying to find ways of dealing with and overcoming life's many challenges. Relationships usually top the list, whether it's dealing with a co-worker, a boss or a friend. It might be coping with the prospect of divorce, or how about the challenges of raising children? From the "terrible two's" to the rebellious teens kids can certainly be more than a handful! If not first on the list for most of you, finances rate a strong second. "I'm living from paycheck-to-paycheck...or how will I pay the rent/mortgage, get out of debt or find my next job?" What about "If I get fired?", and the list goes on and on. Am I talking to anybody here? Then of course we are faced with the inevitable—sickness and death - the death of a loved one and even our own mortality.

Life is difficult. Woven in with all the good things life has to offer are these challenges, these difficulties and quite naturally as humans we often ask why? Why me? When I posed that question to my mentor and pastor Dr. A.R. Bernard, his reply was "Why not you?" It was not the response I was looking for, but the mysteries of life and its' meaning are not for this book. What I would like to do is to bring you, the reader to first ACCEPT the fact that life is indeed difficult and we all will face several challenges in life—some life-long. Secondly, BELIEVE that difficulties can be OVERCOME and at the very least MASTERED.

Who said life would be easy?

I thought that this was supposed to be a truth as a child. Given you followed all the *rules*. You know, you grow-up, get married, a wife, kids, the house with the picket fence and so on. Well life has a way of 'kicking in' and while we all experience glimpses of this utopia (if that is your idea of it), then other things kick in, like dealing with people for one, and the unexpected being the other!

As Pastor Bernard put it, "life is a constant battle for territory". What does that mean? For one, as soon as we are born we fight age. The very elements of life that sustain us, also wear on us. For instance, the sun warms us—but it also ages our skin and wrinkles it with time. Gravity keeps us centered and from floating off into space—but over the years it pulls and tugs at our limbs. Certain parts of our body sag and stretch, food replenishes us—but what if we eat too much, or better yet, what if we are eating too much of the wrong things?! Look, we can spend the rest of this book focused on all the negatives, but we are not going to do that. Just understand life is not always meant to be easy. Why? I don't know. Now the bible, specifically Jesus, talks about giving its believers life more abundantly—but if I recall, the word *easy* is only mentioned once in this voluminous work of 66 books:

"...Take my yoke upon you and learn from me, for I am gentle and humble in heart and you will find rest for your souls. For my yoke is easy and my burden is light..."

Matthew 11:29 NIV

In the book of Matthew in the New Testament, Jesus is obviously talking to some folks who are having a little difficulty dealing with life's problems. Sound familiar? What was true back then is certainly true right here and now.

Throughout the chapters of this book I will reveal the ultimate weapon we are given against difficulty and that is the POWER OF THE SPOKEN WORD.

I am in no way attempting to push a way of life or belief on anyone who reads this book—but I am certainly making available what I have come to accept and believe to be the only fool-proof method of dealing with life's difficulties and that is through scriptures of the BIBLE that provide an ANSWER to EVERY question—every problem known to man.

My life is certainly not an open book nor will I make it one in this writing, but I will reveal parts of myself through my own periods of challenges in life and how the spoken word and scriptures helped changed situations and circumstances. While I put some of my own personal experience out there to give you hope for you to know and understand that you are not alone or unique, I will tell you some real-life stories of other people who have used scripture and the written word to transform their lives. (Of course names have been changed to protest the innocent).

These stories will hit home. I guarantee you will be able to relate to them and perhaps see yourself in some of these scenarios. I believe the only way to touch the minds of people who face difficulties—or who are trying to find any answer in life-is if they can relate to the individual who is trying to help them.

The spoken word coupled with biblical scripture. Can this really be a foundation for dealing with life's difficulties? The answer is yes! As I mentioned earlier, not all difficulties are meant to go away. There are some things that will continue to challenge us throughout our lives. They are called "thorns" and I will explain more about that later in the book. One thing I have learned living on this planet for a half century—NO ONE holds the key to the mystery of this thing called life. Only GOD holds the key and last I heard he has not given it away.

You can sit on a therapist's couch from now until doomsday or seek the truth though millions of self-help books that promise nirvana, but it will never be attained. What the spoken word and scripture will do for you is provide a ROAD MAP for PEACE through the storms of life. Just like the weather, storms will come in your life. You can't stop them. You don't know where they come from at times. One truth—one revelation in this mystery called life that God does provide for us is that there is shelter from life's storms. There is an escape from the cold. There is protection from the wind. There is an umbrella from the rain.

Take this walk with me and Dr. A R. Bernard. Read the stories. Laugh and cry with us as you turn the pages. Apply the power of the spoken word and biblical scriptures you read in this book and you will see a change.

Be ready for something quite different here. Hope does spring eternal!

Julian M. Phillips

CHAPTER ONE

"STICKS and STONES..."

—⚏—

"Hit those turkeys hard man! I mean, knock the living hell out of 'em! You can hit 'em high or low, but hit 'em hard! Those turkeys don't stand a chance when you let 'em know who you are and what you're bringing to the table. Level those son's of b-----s out there!"

I could not explain it, but every time Mr. Burgess came and filled in as a substitute coach for our Pop Warner football team the "Springfield Rifles", we would always play better! It was a practice session on a part grass, part dirt football field at Montbellier Park in the Springfield Gardens section of Queens, New York and I was playing the defensive line. Now I wasn't the biggest kid or the best—but Mr. Burgess' words always seemed to make me play ten times above my level! One of our star running backs, Mike Robinson was about twice my size, but I remember hitting him head on and while he dragged me for what seemed like an eternity, I held on until other players came to my aid and brought him down. I must have made 5 solo tackles that fall afternoon and could sense the eyes of head coach Mr. Ernie following my play most of that day.

I went home feeling good! My uniform was dirty and that was satisfaction enough, knowing good and well I wouldn't see the light of day for a real game. Deep down inside, I felt justified that I was good enough to get playing time, even though Mr. Ernie never put me in the game unless I begged him to do so with minutes left in the 4th quarter. In fact all of the "scrubs" as we were called ran after Mr. Ernie at the end of the game looking to get in so they could go home with a little dirt on their uniforms. It was a badge of honor in a sense that you at least were on the field of battle—if only for a while. The bellowing voice—the words of Mr. Burgess, or Mr. "B" as we affectionately called him made all the difference. Maybe I'm wrong, but it seemed Mr. "B" sensed something greater in me as an athlete than Mr. Ernie did. Mr. "B's voice—his words always inspired me to play above my potential—or at least I thought at the time.

Now Mr. "B" was a big man. He worked for the New York City Sanitation Department picking up garbage for a living. Every now and then he worked the streets of our middle- class black neighborhood in St. Albans, Queens.

You could hear that huge truck a block away, the sound of those big brakes screeching to a halt every time a garbage can was picked up in front of somebody's house. The clang of an empty can as the workers threw it to the concrete and then the engines again in full blast racing toward the next house. It was the routine three days a week and not much of a big deal except for when Mr. "B" was on the route. I would run out to see him bark orders to his crew. It was like he was on the football field firing off words of inspiration. Mr. "B" took pride in his job and the routine of picking up garbage turned into an adventure when he was on the scene.

For years, I could not figure out what made me play better when Mr. "B" was coaching the team, or why I was so drawn to his personality. I would often think back to those days on that dirt and grass field inside Montbellier Park during periods of self-doubt in my life. Why could I rise above the challenge? How was it the head coach could never 'push the right buttons' and Mr. "B" could? Well after listening to a few sermons from Dr. A.R. Bernard in the early nineties the light went on. It was Mr. "B's WORDS! Put aside the occasional profanity, Mr. "B" was ALWAYS POSITIVE. He made you BELIEVE you could accomplish the task. No matter how big the giant, Mr. "B's focus was on us—not the opposition.

In life there always has been a person, a leader with the right WORDS to inspire people to become something, endure a great hardship or propel them to victory, despite overwhelming odds. I look to some of history's great leaders as prime examples. Take British Prime Minister Sir Winston Churchill's first speech to the nation on the brink of war facing a seemingly unstoppable Nazi war machine blazing across Europe. The very survival of the tiny island nation in jeopardy:

"...We have before us many, many months of struggle and suffering. You ask, what is our policy? I say it is to wage war by land and sea, and air. War with all our might and with all the strength God had given us and to wage war against a monstrous tyranny never surpassed in the dark and lamentable catalogue of human crime. That is our policy. You ask, what is our aim? I can answer in one word. It is victory. Victory at all costs-victory in spite of all terrors-victory however long and hard the road may be, for without victory there is no survival..."

Sir Winston Churchill before the House of Commons
May 13, 1940

Many consider this to be one of the greatest call-to-arms ever uttered and I certainly agree. These WORDS mobilized an entire nation. More importantly, they inspired and strengthened the spirits of people who surely had fear in their hearts with all of the devastating news they heard about the Nazis. However, despite that inspiring speech, less than one month later as the Nazis pressed the fight, moving closer to England's shores, the peril and the possibility of defeat surely seemed a reality. On May 26th, Operation Dynamo began. This was the evacuation of thousands of British troops from the beaches of Dunkirk. It was a retreat no doubt and the prospect of an annihilation of a large part of their ground forces by the powerful German Luftwaffe air force. God certainly has a way of working things out though. The seas were calm and other factors came into play to avoid a disaster. Faced with this situation, Churchill delivered this speech to the House of Commons:

"...Even though large tracts of Europe and many old and famous states have fallen into the grip of the Gestapo and all the odious apparatus of Nazi rule ,we shall not flag or fail. We shall go on to the end, we shall fight in France, we shall fight on the seas and the oceans, we shall fight with growing confidence and growing strength in the air, we shall defend our island whatever the cost may be, we shall fight on the beaches, we shall fight on the landing grounds, we shall fight in the fields and in the streets, we shall fight in the hills, we shall never surrender, and even if, which I do not for a moment believe, this island or a large part of it were subjugated and starving, then our empire beyond the seas, armed and guarded by the British fleet, would carry on the struggle, until, in God's good time, the new world, with all its power and might steps forth to rescue and liberate the old.."

Sir Winston Churchill before the House of Commons
June 4th 1940

What powerful words! With all that England faced, it took the WORDS of one man to give the nation hope.

What is it about words that can dramatically change a person's world? Now, what words can do in the positive — unfortunately they can also do in the negative.

Because of years of promises unfulfilled and racism in the early part of the 20th century, my father became a very bitter man. As a result, he handed down that negativity to the rest of the family. *"You can never do this, or you can never do that"* were the daily words of 'inspiration' in my house. The one phrase I remember the most as a kid was, *"You better enjoy these days now, because when you get older it will all be downhill"*.

No wonder my sister and I had serious self esteem problems that we carried into adulthood! Words have a way of impacting us, either in a positive way or in a negative way. Can you imagine being fed positive words? Words that build you up instead of tearing you down? Words that give you hope and strength? Mr. "B" worked wonders through his WORDS. Winston Churchill led a nation through its darkest hours by his WORDS.

The old phrase we used to say as kids growing up, *'sticks and stones can break my bones, but words will never harm me'* was and is so far from the truth!

How do you use words? What words do you draw upon in times of need? Words stated and written by great leaders like Sir Winston Churchill and others can be helpful and I do rely on them from time-to time. You can look up famous speeches and quotes in books and computers when you are searching for encouragement—but more importantly THE WORD uttered by God is far more important than any uttered by man!

WORDS

Thank God for language, the ability to communicate, to turn on thoughts from the unseen and then into the visible realm.

Words are the most powerful things. It is through words the Bible says God created the universe. He spoke it into existence. The Bible reveals that everything is upheld by the word of his power. So His word carries, sustains, creates everything. Just as God's creative power is in His words, our creative power is in our words. Through our words we create joy, we create sadness, we create pain, we create relationships. We express ideas and visions and dreams through our words. Our lives are constructed by our words. So that makes words the most powerful tool that we have in human relationships.

*God's word has power in and of itself. Jesus spoke that words are containers. They carry life, they carry death, they carry healing, they carry hurt. He made reference to the old testament passage in the book of Proverbs that says death and life are in the power of the tongue (**Proverbs 18:21**), and* *whatever words we speak, whether words of life or words of death, we'll eat the fruit of those words. So words are carriers. Words are the expression of thought. Words, when meditated on can go from the ear, to the mind into the heart and can revolutionize our lives, our thinking—or put us in prisons, because those words, they strip us of our self esteem, our self worth, or those words may empower us. You take the young child who grows up in a home where the mother is a bitter and single parent, abandoned by the father and her husband and instead of forgiving and releasing her bitterness, she harbors it. So out of a bitter heart, comes bitter words and that bitterness is communicated to that child. That child can be told 'don't trust anybody' 'no one really loves you' 'people will betray you' 'you're never going to amount to anything'. As a result, that child after hearing that over and over again, while it is not true, it can become their perception of themselves and their living reality. Words have that kind of power.*

HEALING

In the book of Psalms it says God's response to the human condition is that he sent His word to heal them and deliver them from destruction. As Christians, we believe in the biblical revelation that says that he took His word of healing, of redemption, of reconciliation, and He gave it a body. That body was incarnation which is Jesus Christ. So what Jesus did in opening blind eyes, unstopping deaf ears, raising the dead, causing the lame to walk, the dumb to speak—that was simply God's healing word incarnated and producing the very results He intended.

When we talk about psychosomatic illness, we understand that whatever the mind cannot contain—and it's usually in words, that it will impose itself on the body. So just as the mind that is overwhelmed with worry and fear and anxiety which is the result of something it heard, which are words— the body then begins to take upon itself that stress and it is manifested in sickness and disease. The reverse of that is also true. If that mind is occupied, implanted with words and thoughts and beauty and wholesomeness—words that are positive and uplifting—then it will have a positive and uplifting effect upon the body.

In James Allen's book As a Man Thinketh, where he says "as a man thinketh in his heart, so is he", is so true. When you talk about thinking, you talk about processing words in a systematic way intended to gain some result.

God, in giving Joshua the mandate of leadership in the passing of Moses, gave him specific instructions. Here's a man that was to lead over a million people into their promised land they would have to literally—even though they were untrained as warriors, go against very powerful nations. And in the key instructions that God gave him, He said this book of law is simply the words that God gave to Moses. He told Joshua, He said this book of the law shall not depart out of your mouth. Which means that you will make it a constant flow from your lips. That you shall meditate therein day and night. That you may observe to do all that is written there. That you may prosper and have good success. So here he is a leader—and what does God refer him to for success? The words that God gave to his servant Moses. And He said that if you meditate on those words (and to meditate means to speak to yourself) you then become empowered in such a way that you'll successfully lead these people into their promised land.

Dr. A.R. Bernard

Here are some scriptures I draw upon in times of need that may be of help to you. Read them. Recite them out loud. Meditate on them daily or more if needed. Make these words in the scriptures a part of who you are! They are the promises of God. If you are skeptical, just go with the flow for once. I guarantee you, you will get results!

May God bless you in this exercise.

Note: All scriptures taken from Holy Bible, New International Version (NIV)

Remember: *The tongue* (word/s) *has the power of life and death...* NIV

Proverbs Chapter 18 verse 21 (Old Testament)

Ephesians Chapter 3 verse 16:
I pray that out of his glorious riches he may strengthen you with his power through his Spirit in your inner being. NIV (Old Testament)

Psalm 27 verses 1-3
The Lord is my light and my salvation—whom shall I fear? The Lord is the stronghold of my life—of whom shall I be afraid? When evil men advance against me to devour my flesh, when enemies and my foes attack me, they will stumble and fall. Though an army besiege me, my heart will not fear, though wars break out against me, even then will I be confident! NIV (Old Testament)

Psalm 39 verse 7
But now Lord, what do I look for? My hope is in you. Save me from all my transgressions. NIV (Old Testament)

CHAPTER TWO

FALSE EVIDENCE

—ɯ—

Tobias sat in his easy chair peering out of his first floor window at the West End Apartments in Brooklyn, clutching a 12 oz. can of Budweiser. Now I can't remember the exact day, but it must have been a weekend, because the TV was on with sports blaring in the background and outside in the courtyard, people were making their way to and from the guard booth with huge bundles of clothes for the laundry or carrying large plastic and paper bags from the supermarket.

I always spent a lot of time down in Tobias' apartment almost any day of the week, drinking beers with the fellas and smoking a joint. Marijuana, alcohol and cocaine were the popular drugs of choice for the 'in crowd' during the 70's and 80's, but this time was different. His wife and son were not home. None of the usual guys were on hand to suck down a few beers or partake in other sinful delights.

It was just Tobias and me. He called me because he wanted to talk and I figured if Tobias wanted to talk about something, it must be important. As I sat down ready to listen, the tears ran down his face. The words came out of his mouth stunned me and changed my perspective on how I looked at people forever.

"Julian, don't you ever tell anybody I told you this, but I'm scared to death!"

Tobias scared to death? Tobias was bigger than life. He stood about 6 feet 6. He was light skinned and very muscular and had a commanding voice. Tobias grew up in South Carolina and made sure everybody knew it! He was proud of his southern roots and always said he would go back home someday. Everybody knew him in the complex, I mean if you did not see him you could certainly hear him inside the courtyard engaged in a casual conversation with a neighbor or witness him 'policing' the complex grounds of unruly teens. Tobias seemed fearless. He worked in construction. Had hands bigger than mallets and when it came to security at West End, I would have bet my last money on him over the security guards we paid well to keep the peace around the place. I could not fathom Tobias being scared about anything! But as I mentioned in the last chapter, life has a way of 'kicking in' and for Tobias, his massive size and authoritative voice masked the fear within. The alcohol and drugs were a smokescreen (like they are for many of us) for the things that he feared most. The question - what was Tobias so afraid of?

Tobias was married to a wonderful woman named Brenda. Unlike him, she was quiet in nature and was raised up north. They were certainly opposites in many ways. Brenda was a professional woman, who held a job at a prestigious firm on Wall Street and always dressed the part. Tobias has a child from another woman years before he married Brenda named Bret who was now in his teens. Now on the surface, they looked like any other family trying to put the pieces together to make a living—and in fact they were. Tobias and Brenda both shared the dream of owning their own home. Bret was a bright kid who didn't always apply himself in high school but accomplished enough to get by and was looking to go to college. Sounds good? Well things started to change a few years back when Tobias could not find steady work in construction. During the 'good' times, the paychecks were big, the money was rolling in and with Brenda's salary they did pretty well. But without those big paychecks, things started to change—for the worse! Tobias could not always make ends meet and the very thought of this proud southern man trading his morning ride to work for a trip to the unemployment office was, well you know way too much for his ego.

The confrontations began with Brenda. I'm not sure whether anything ever turned physical, but things definitely got ugly. Brenda never seemed to mind that Tobias worked in construction; however without that steady paycheck…Tobias often mentioned that he felt Brenda would have preferred a 'professional' man. Perhaps he was projecting, but nevertheless the thought was real in his mind. Don't think for a minute these confrontations did not affect Bret. They lived in a small two-bedroom apartment. He could hear the arguments. On top of that, Bret was now a teenager trying to make sense of a world that was changing to him. He traded his love for toys and companionship with his friends for girls. Bret was becoming a man now — at least in his own mind and now you have two 'bulls' under one roof. Get the picture? Tobias wanted the best for his son. He was a good father, but perhaps pushed his will on his son more than he should have.

Tobias did not know any better but the 'my way or the highway' mentality did not work well with Bret. On the other hand no steady job and the reality of a marriage coming apart at the seams were too much for Tobias to bear.

Had life boiled down to this? Suddenly Tobias felt trapped in a cage with no way out. No hope. Who could he turn to? For me, the very thought that a man like Tobias was afraid kind of threw me for a loop. What kind of advice could I give him? I certainly was not involved in church, nor did I have any relationship with God—at least not the one I have now.

"Everything will work out fine Tobias. You will find work and things will be good between you and Brenda, just wait and see" I said. As for Bret, "he's a good kid," I went on. "You need to let him find his way by giving him the right to make his own choices. That does not mean you stop being a father by providing the discipline and guidance he needs." Tobias clutched that can of Budweiser even harder to the point it crumbled in his hands. He did not say another word. I sat there with him for what seemed like an eternity. We both peered out into the courtyard. I thought about my own life, my fears. What was I afraid of?

For most of us, life's daily challenges stir up fears. Fears, mostly about what the next day is going to bring. We simply don't know the future, although we spend a lot of time thinking or worrying about it. To an extent, we all have our coping devices. Some of us look at the daily horoscope in the newspaper while on the way to work, hoping to find some clue as to what the next 24 hours will bring. Sadly, some shape our day around what the horoscope says. If it's good, fantastic! We believe we will meet that significant other, or find a hot date or perhaps make that business deal. Ok not so bad. I'm always supportive of positive thinking—but what if the horoscope does not provide good news?

From the horoscope to fortune telling, to talking to a friend, relative, a therapist or drowning our fears in drugs—not knowing what the future holds can create a lot of fear in folks. Now you don't have to be facing bad times like Tobias to know fear. The prospect of getting married can bring on fear. Is this the right person? Will it last? How about the

birth of a child and all of a sudden becoming a parent? What about that new job or promotion and the increased responsibilities that will surely go with it? The list goes on and on. Fear, something we all deal with in our lives. The question is, how do we get off this not so merry-go-round that enslaves us all too often?

F.E.A.R. (False Evidence Appears Real)

Fear affects the spirit, the soul and the body. With the mind processing some danger, some unknown, the first reaction is what we call fear apprehension. When it become obsessive, it becomes a phobia in our lives and it could be of anything. But fear has strength because of a lack of knowledge. What we don't know or understand, we tend to fear. So knowledge is the beginning of expelling fear. But there is something greater than that and it is called love. I say it's greater because you can love without understanding. You can intuitively feel safety, security, peace under someone's covering. And there is that knowledge that is intuitive that results in that feeling of assurance and confidence. The Bible says with regard to fear, fear came as a result of man leaving that safety of relationship with God and entering this realm of human experience, this universe, apart from the source of knowledge. So what man could have known by his connection with God, he now has to discover. Remember, the tree is the tree of the knowledge of good and evil, so obviously he (man) had the knowledge of good which was God. But God shielded man from the knowledge of evil by commanding man not to eat from that tree. Man was informed by that command that it existed, but he didn't have knowledge of it, and in the Bible the word knowledge, or to know someone, speaks of it on an intimate level. So as a result, his hunger and pursuit for knowledge through disobedience to God put him in a position where he realized his human frailty and his nakedness, his shame. And that he really did not measure up to the vastness of this universe and fear set in. The fear of the unknown, the fear of his destiny, the fear of death, the fear of all of those things that now began to dominate his life although he was designed to have dominion over it. God's answer to that is love. The Bible reveals that there is no fear in love and it is so true, because when you're convinced that someone loves you, you are not afraid of them. When you are convinced that someone loves you, you trust their protection. There is a confidence that dispels fear and as that knowledge or understanding of love matures, the assurance becomes stronger in your life and you get to a place where you don't need evidence of it any longer. You just know. That is liberating.

I would lead them (readers) to God's love. For God so loved the world that he gave His only begotten son which was Christ. The Christ came, and as you read the gospels conquered all the things that we fear; sickness, disease, death, power, the unknown, the demonic, famine. Everything that we could possibly fear as humans he demonstrated his authority over it, his dominion over it. And the ultimate dominion is where he rose from the dead in that he conquered the fear of death.

The reader of this book may be a Christian, may be a Buddhist, may be a Muslim, may be a Hindu, which are all religions, because it is religion that tries to explain God. I hold personally to the Christian faith because it is not a faith that has been discovered by human ingenuity. It is something that has been revealed. So it's a revealed faith. And that faith reveals that there is someone greater than myself, greater than all human power and that individual loves me, cares for me, has my past, present, and future in their control. And nothing happens in my life without their plan or their permission. You have to have someone or something greater than yourself because you know your own human frailty and weakness. And once you have trust in someone greater than yourself, greater than any power that could ever be imagined—ultimate power, ultimate reality—and you trust that they'll always have your best interest at heart then you enter a place of peace.

Dr. A.R. Bernard

I don't know about you, but I still struggle with fear to this day. You can't stop the spirit of fear from trying to attack you, just like you can't stop the rain falling from the sky. However, you can put up an umbrella to protect you from that rain. It's the same with fear. There has to come a point when you realize there are some things we can control and there are other things we can't. For the most part we let fear into our lives over things we have absolutely no control over. You have to constantly remind yourself and TELL yourself to let go. The future is a mystery. You certainly can do your best to prepare for it—but ultimately the chips always fall in a way that have nothing to do with your best intentions or preparation. I deal with the future by trying not to think about it. Now trying not to think about the future does not always work, I'm human! But my trump card is God. I GO to Him for help. I ASK Him for advice. I SEEK Him for wisdom. I may not always get an answer right away, but one thing I have is the comfort of KNOWING there is something much greater than myself that has my best interests at heart. So far after 50 years of facing fear, I've managed to survive and at times thrive. I look back on some of the things I was fearful of at the time and laugh. Why was I so afraid? Fear sometimes tries to bring me back to my past. It is Satan's way of trying to enslave us. Keep pressing forward no matter the challenge for the goal is nothing less than VICTORY. Refer back to chapter one and the words of Sir Winston Churchill.

If you were wondering about Tobias' family, I have not seen them in years, but I understand all is well in their household these days. Life did had a way of 'kicking in'—but so did God's word.

When you are facing fear, recite these scriptures. They have helped me and I know they will be of great comfort to your mind and soul. Remember, God's word is his power. It is also YOUR power. Go to these as often as you need. Like medicine, the Word may not take effect immediately, but unlike worldly medicine, it WILL take effect. Give it time!

May God bless.

Suggested scriptures

Philippians Chapter 4 verses 6&7
Do not be anxious about anything, but in everything, by prayer and petition, with thanksgiving, present your requests to God. And the peace of God, which transcends all understanding, will guard your hearts and minds.... NIV (New Testament)

Proverbs Chapter 3 verses 5&6
Trust in the Lord with all your heart and lean not on your own understanding; in all your ways acknowledge him, and he will make your paths straight. NIV (Old Testament)

Isaiah Chapter 43 verses 1-3
Fear not, for I have redeemed you: I have summoned you by name; you are mine. When you pass through the waters, I will be with you; and when you pass through the rivers, they will not sweep over you. When you walk through the fire, you will not be burned; the flames will not set you ablaze. For I am the Lord, your God, the **Holy One** *of Israel, your Savior..."* NIV (Old Testament)

Philippians Chapter 4 verse 13
I can do everything through Him who gives me strength.
NIV (New Testament)

CHAPTER THREE

THE SUBSTITUTE

—〰—

I slowly made my way up the steps to the big wooden front door of our brownstone on Fortune Avenue in Brooklyn. It was a late afternoon and I had spent the day at a close friend's house in New Jersey waiting for the impending doom. For months my wife Barbara and I had talked about this day. The day she said she was leaving. Joint counseling sessions didn't seem to help. My reasoning and pleading for a change of mind did not make any difference either. After nearly thirteen years of marriage, Barbara wanted a separation plain and simple!

Perhaps it was my success as a reporter for WNBC-TV in New York that was a factor for her. As great singer as she was, her career had not taken off at the time while mine perhaps seemed to be moving quite rapidly in the right direction. Maybe another reason might have been because she had never lived on her own, except for four years spent pursuing a psychology degree at Vassar College in upstate Poughkeepsie, New York.

As I was climbing up those steps—which seemed like a trek up Mount Everest at the time, a lot of reasons for the separation started to cross my mind. For one, we had a failed pregnancy. After numerous consultations with doctors, the likelihood of having any children in the future was remote. There were no concrete answers as to why this was not possible. Needless to say this played heavily on her mind for months. Then there were my issues. My issues? Don't think for one minute Mr. Julian Phillips himself was not a factor in all of this! I was not the best person with money. Let's just say I was a horrible manager of finances! Where do we start with this money nightmare? Well for one, Barbara and I had a joint American Express account. I can't even remember how long it took, but after a lot of overspending and just plain mismanagement, our account was canceled and our credit was compromised. This was a big deal for her—and it should have been for me also. Forget about my credit, but screw-up Barbara's credit?! I think you are starting to get the picture. There were a lot of *issues* in 'Camelot', and one day Barbara sat down and said to me *"I've been Julian's wife, my parents' kid and I feel dead"*.

I slipped the copper key into the cylinder of the front door and slowly opened it up. Looking straight up the carpeted stairs to the second floor was a familiar face smiling with her tongue hanging out like nothing was wrong. It was our dog Miko. She was a big black and white Japanese Akita. Dogs have a way of taking the edge off of things. No matter the circumstance they are forever faithful, but this day was different. I ignored Miko's licks and walked past her to the bedroom. Barbara's closets were empty. I cased the entire house and there wasn't a trace of Barbara except for the coat closet downstairs. She left a few coats behind, but I realized they were left because she could not take everything with her. I thumbed through what she left behind. Basically, she left the non-essentials. The bathroom cabinet was stripped of her personal items. At this point I realized I was alone. After about an hour of sitting in the empty brownstone with Miko pacing back and forth, we both went out for a walk. Somehow we managed to make it to the liquor store and I bought a bottle of sparkling wine. That night I called Barbara where she was spending the night with a girlfriend and begged her to come back home. Somehow I knew my pleas for reconciliation would not be nearly enough. Years of doubt and unfulfilled promises took center stage and our marriage was in serious jeopardy. Worry began to rear its' ugly head. How was I going to handle the house?

After all, Barbara juggled all of the bills. All I did was hand over the paycheck to her. I realized I didn't have a clue. It was a bitter pill to swallow and admit that at least part of the reasons for the break-up had do with my inability to take responsibility as a husband. I downed that bottle of sparkling wine and went to sleep. Let's say that bottle was my only friend. An empty bed only a reminder of what once was.

East 42nd street at lunchtime is a very busy place. Heck, it's busy most of the time, but I felt I was living in a ghost town the day after Barbara left. Nothing seemed to exist except CitiBank on the corner of Lexington and 42nd Street. It was two blocks from my job and I walked into the front door and asked to see a manager. The folks at the information booth directed me to a tiny partitioned area. It was a small office with a window that faced 42nd street. I peered out for a moment watching people go by. Gripped by yesterday's events, the tears came rolling down my cheeks. "May I help you?" a woman asked. I turned around to see the branch manager staring down at me. "My wife has left me and I don't know how to balance a check book. Can you help me?"

The spirit of worry had taken full effect. It's easy to see why. Now I was not going to beat up on myself at this point about the worry issue because there was already a lot on my plate! Can somebody cut me some slack here? The most important thing I didn't realize was that worry was not going to cut me any slack. The more I worried, the worse things in my mind got. It was a vicious cycle. Worry lead to more worry and anxiety. What dawned on me was that despite the current set of circumstances, worry was a part of my entire life. Where do we start? The constant negativity handed down from a bitter father that I mentioned earlier in the book? That perhaps might be a good start. But like most of us, I could point to a million things that triggered worry and fear in my life. You know these two maladies go hand-in-hand. The issue at this point, this cross-road in my life was what to do about it. How do I get past this without it consuming me?

WORRY

Worry is a negative child of fear. Fear gives birth to worry. And worry becomes a negative response to fear. The reason why we call it a substitute is because you're worrying instead of doing something else. What is that something else you should be doing? And in our faith tradition, that something else is prayer. So worry becomes a substitute for prayer. And it's because you're not trusting in someone greater than yourself, and because you're conscious of your own inadequacies and human frailties then you know trusting in yourself is a possibility of failure.

THE POWER OF PRAYER

The power behind prayer is what it reveals. It reveals that God is personal. He is not a rock, a stone, a tree. He is not something that cannot respond, or cannot be touched by the feeling of our weakness in our struggle. That is so important. Prayer says that God hears. God processes what I'm saying and God responds. So knowing that he hears me, I can be confident that he'll respond, whether that response is a yes a no or a wait. Prayer makes God a personal God, which means like me He reflects, He thinks ahead as well. He processes things through thought and emotion. He is not removed from me and my experience.

WAITING FOR ANSWER TO PRAYER

Wait is an active word, it is not passive. Wait is the time period in which you have the opportunity to exercise your faith. You're faced with a choice to embrace your doubts or hold on to your faith. Without that practice, you'll never experience the perseverance or the acceptance that God is sovereign, that God knows more than us. We don't accept that there is a time for everything in life, that we discover all of these things in the waiting process.

Dr. A.R. Bernard

In case you are wondering, Barbara and I got back together! I got my act together with the money thing. I take care of most of the finances now. We renewed our wedding vows and moved to a house on Long Island where we have been together for the past eight years. As of this writing Barbara has completed her debut CD.

Faith brought us back together and that will be the subject of the next chapter, but let's focus on this issue of worry. Worry had no influence as to whether Barbara and I got back together or not. In fact worry will not affect destiny. It will not affect anything but your physical and mental health. Worry is designed to destroy you! Like fear, we usually worry about the things we simply have no control over. Your choices, your decisions and God's plan for your life are the only things that affect your destiny.

If you find yourself worrying about something, just ask yourself this simple question. Will my worrying about this situation change anything? The answer is a resounding no! Try to come up with a plan of action for what might be worrying you. Make a decision. Make a choice. But most of all, when you are faced with worry and don't know what to do, PRAY! **Worry is a substitute for prayer!**

Here are some suggested scriptures to recite for comfort when worried, and to pray over.

Grace and peace.

Psalm 138 verses 7& 8
Though I walk in the midst of trouble, you preserve my life; you stretch out your hand against the anger of my foes, with your right hand you save me. The Lord will **fulfill** *his purpose for me....* NIV (Old Testament)

Psalm 119 verse114
You are my refuge and my shield; I have put my hope in your word. NIV (Old Testament)

Matthew Chapter 6 verse 25-27
Therefore I tell you, do not worry about your life, what you will eat or drink; or about your body, what you will wear. Is not life more important than clothes? Look at the birds of the air; they do not sow or reap or store away in barns, and yet your heavenly Father feeds them. Are you not much more valuable than they? Who of you by worrying can add a single hour to his life? NIV (New Testament)

Psalm 23 (Old Testament)
Meditate on the entire passage!

1 Corinthians Chapter 2 verse 9
"No eye has seen, no ear has heard, no mind has conceived what God has prepared for those who love him" NIV (New Testament)

CHAPTER FOUR

"WE'VE COME THIS FAR..."

After five years of walking with the Lord a lot happened in my life for the better. After all, Barbara was back and I worried less about *things*. My relationship with Pastor A.R. Bernard grew closer. But being the skeptic that I am, I was still wary of this man that God placed in my life. He helped me through a troubled marriage. He guided me through the pain and anguish of my mother's death. He helped me with issues of worry and fear. The thing that bothered me about Pastor Bernard was that he seemed to have all the answers that I was looking for. My thing was I knew he wasn't God and he must have some flaws. I was preparing myself for an eventual letdown. After all the negative stuff that plagued me a good part of my life—and never having a real father/mentor relationship growing up, I figured there would be something looming down the road that would end this relationship in a bad way. Come on, I'm human! Like God's chosen people, all the miracles in the world were not enough to convince them of His mighty power.

Pastor taught that God is a relationship God and he works with us in many ways, but often through people. One evening I invited Pastor Bernard over to our house for dinner. It was one of those times I was in mental anguish and I needed to talk. He came. During the evening he revealed that he was *assigned* to me by God. Assigned? What the heck did that mean? "You're only interested in me because I'm a well known reporter," I respectfully barked back. Pastor paused with a look of I don't know what on his face and said,"Do you know how busy I am"? Needless to say, after all he had done, I felt a little more than embarrassed and apologized.

After dinner, we talked for a while about a lot of things, mainly purpose and destiny. You see, I had this concern, this *worry* about my future. After years of reporting on the streets of New York, first at WNBC-TV, WCBS-TV and then WPIX-TV I was ready for another challenge, I wanted to sit in the anchor chair and get off the streets. The problem was I was constantly getting overlooked. It was completely insane to me. I hosted three talk shows in my career. Two at WNBC and a public affairs series at WPIX called "Best Talk". One year "Best Talk" was nominated and won an award as the best public affairs show in New York State. During my time at WPIX my boss and good friend to this day, Karen Scott, gave me the job of co-hosting the station's national July 4th fireworks broadcasts and even the Puerto Rican Day Parade telecast which I'm told was the highest rated in the history of the station's coverage of this spectacle. In my mind the ratings spoke for themselves. I was popular and when the openings came up for the weekend anchor job and the new morning show, I was certain I'd be a shoe-in! Come on, I was not the only one who felt that way. I got a lot of support from my peers for either spot, but when the announcements came down for both jobs, yours truly did not make the cut.

Was it pride or something deeper inside me that felt I could do better? After a few hours Pastor Bernard reminded me that God had a plan for my life and that somebody who would make a difference is, and will be watching. Hogwash! I said to myself. Pastor was wrong on this one. Nobody wanted me, not even other stations I sent audition tapes to. I had fired my agent a few years before and I could not find another one that would represent me. Was I blackballed? I couldn't figure out why. The fact was, as good as I thought I was—nobody seemed interested. I was finally willing to accept I might be a legend in my own mind and that is what I told Pastor that night. After he left, his words about somebody watching kept playing over and over again in my head. Was Pastor right on this issue as he had been on so many others in my life in the past? Like in a game of craps somehow I felt the dice would eventually roll snake eyes. It all boiled down to trust. Something I had a big problem with. Forget about Pastor, I wanted to hear from God himself! Not getting any signs from the Supreme Being that night I finally went to sleep.

Before daybreak I was awakened by a huge thunderstorm. You gotta understand, nothing, I mean nothing ever disturbs my sleep—but this one night was different. Now my wife Barbara did not flinch through it all. This was weird because the slightest noise usually brings her out of a deep sleep. But there she was, curled up like a little angel, while I'm running around the house sweating and my heart feeling like it was trying to bust out of my chest! Was it God trying to tell me something? I thought for a moment about trust and this thing Pastor often talked about called **faith.**

Four years had passed since that night Pastor stopped by for dinner and I still was at WPIX reporting on the streets. By this time I could mail-in the stories. It became that routine—and boring. To make matters even worse, the station no longer had the broadcast rights to the parades, or the fireworks telecast. The final nail in the coffin for me was the cancellation of "Best Talk". It was my only refuge from the streets. My desk was placed in a cubby hole next to the copy machine in the newsroom. One of my colleagues whom I often spoke with and who knew my ambitions said, "I've heard this talk from you about wanting to anchor for several years now. Face it, you'll die in this job like the rest of us here."

Nine years in a job and station where I thought I'd only stay for one three-year contract. I was a broken man, a mere shell of myself. I tried to have faith. I tried to believe beyond what I saw and was feeling. Faith was one thing—but reality was saying something totally different. Could it be that this was the end of the road? A journeyman reporter with nothing more to look forward to in my career? While my love for God was always there, church became nothing more than a routine. A place to go to help master my anxieties about life and relationships. A place to listen, sing songs of worship and praise, submit an offering and hear the Word. Pastor was getting so busy and popular; it was becoming increasingly hard to get his attention. Perhaps that was good in a way, because I really did not like having to depend on him—or anyone for that matter. I had a huge problem with this trust and faith thing. I figured if you did good work you would eventually be rewarded. However, life is not always fair and I was slowly beginning to accept that reality.

Boredom took a back seat to the biggest story of my career, when those two planes struck the twin towers at the World Trade Center on September 11th 2001. Life as we knew it in the free-world changed forever. We were in a sense no longer free. Terrorism would be a way of life to Americans in the 21st century, just like the cold war was for the world in the 20th century. Personally my life changed, if only for a moment. After what seemed like an eternity, I was once again challenged to perform. There were stories to uncover, people to interview. There was a crisis at hand and for the first time in years I felt I had an opportunity to make a difference. However, about 6 months after that horrible disaster, life for me returned to the way it was—one more boring story after another and more rejections from prospective employers and agents. The only constant at this time was Pastor. He maintained that something good was going to happen. I maintained that he was out of his mind—out of touch with reality in this case.

Out of nowhere it seemed there was a chance that my fortune had turned for the better. I got a call that Michael Bloomberg was looking for advice on his campaign for Mayor of New York City. My good friend Rudy Washington, a former Deputy Mayor with the Giuliani administration suggested me. It didn't take much to accept the offer. Now it might seem selfish and I must admit that it was, but Bloomberg was a multi-billionaire. He had connections and deep pockets. At the very least I thought he might help me for helping him, even if he lost. Well, the meeting was arranged and I spent the better part of four plus hours on a golf course trading shots with one of the most powerful men in the world and it was time well spent! I convinced him that he should spend a considerable amount of time courting the black vote by visiting churches in those communities. Bloomberg seemed reluctant at first. "Will they accept me?" he said. "Black people are not monolithic," I responded. "Even though most blacks in this town are Democrats and you are a Republican and much is not known about you— if you say something they can identify with, you will be accepted." The rest is history. Bloomberg's first visit was to my church, the Christian Cultural Center in Brooklyn. He got a standing ovation. My pastor endorsed him and eventually became friends with the man who would be Mayor. In the meantime I'm waiting for assistance, but nothing happened. I couldn't even get close to The Mayor shortly after the election. What I thought would be my meal ticket turned to slop and I got bitter. I relayed this feeling to Pastor Bernard and he said, "Your relationship with Bloomberg had nothing to do with your personal future. You were being used for a greater purpose to bring him into a relationship with the black community and our churches as a whole. Bloomberg is not the answer for your future. God will take care of you." Within two months I received the opportunity of a lifetime. I was offered the job of weekend anchor at Fox News Channel, the number one cable news network in the country. Imagine this extraordinary change. From street reporter in a local news station to international news anchor and one of only four black male network anchors in the entire country!

FAITH

Faith is the foundation of Christianity as well as the universe! The non religious or the atheist gets on an airplane traveling from one city to another—that is an act of faith. He has no idea who is flying that plane—and if he happens to know the name of the captain, he doesn't know the disposition. There is no guarantee that he will arrive at his destination safely. It's an act of faith. It's an act of faith to step out of your door in the morning—to go about your business, to eat, to believe that what you are eating is going to do the right thing when it goes inside your body, that somehow you know your body is going to break it down and distribute the nutrients and minerals, I mean the whole universe runs on faith. We could not build a society without faith. Faith is that intangible substance of which dreams are made of and visions achieved. We take it from the mind grasping the possibilities. We put it on paper, on architectural drawings and when we bring the brick and mortar, engineers and everyone together and there it is! We started in the realm of faith. We cannot exist as a people without faith. Relationship is based on faith. Forgiveness: There are no guarantees that a person who says that they are sorry is truly sorry. If you issue that forgiveness because you've received that apology, that's an act of faith. No day of our life, no minute of our life is guaranteed. Every bit of what we do is an act of faith.

I think that we can all accept the reality that everyone, believer and non believer—atheist, Christian, we all live in a world that requires faith as the basis for us to live and operate. So the question is not is there faith—the question is what is your faith in? Is your faith in your own power, your money, your love, your health, because if your faith is in those things that have proven over time to be perishable, then that faith is going to be weak and subject to the strength of the thing that is perishable. But if your faith is in God, the Supreme Being, the higher power, someone greater than our mankind, then it gives you a peace, because now you are trusting in the eternal, not the temporal.

THE FAITH CHAPER IN THE BIBLE

Chapter 11 in the book of Hebrews in the New Testament deals with faith. What can go unnoticed in that chapter which has been an imbalance in much of what is taught about faith today in Christian circles is that the beginning of the chapter spoke of heroes — Daniel, Abraham, Joseph, Isaac—who used their faith and experienced incredible victories and deliverances. But in the last portion of that chapter, it speaks of those who were tortured, who were left hungry and destitute, died. And yet God commended them for their faith. So there is the commendation of faith because we see victory. But there is also the commendation of faith for those who suffered defeat, because it took faith and God commended those who were tortured for not allowing the torture to change their faith. For not allowing the famine, the conditions that they were not delivered from to alter their faith. So faith is not just having the thing that you hoped for, but sometimes faith is going through the experience of pain and suffering. That takes faith to not give up and turn away from your beliefs.

Dr. A.R. Bernard

At the time of this writing, three and one half years have passed since joining Fox News Channel. With the vision of Fox CEO Roger Ailes, who had the courage and wisdom to give me a chance, plus God's hand on my life, the Weekend Fox & Friends show became the number one morning weekend cable news show in the country, and remained that way for the years I was added to the show as co-host, along with Mike Jerrick and Juliet Huddy.

The thing is, even though my faith was weak God proved himself worthy. I received positive words and a vision that never changed from my pastor, despite what it looked like. That's faith for you. The substance of things hoped for, the evidence not seen!

The important thing here is that I don't believe it was my faith that made the difference. As you have witnessed my faith at times was very weak. However, it was the undying faith and prayers of my pastor and others who would not let me waiver when the storms got rough and I could not see the light at the end of the tunnel.

Can you believe in this miracle called faith? Do you have the courage to believe in things that are not presently a reality as if they were?

Scriptures to read and recite that increase faith.

Hebrews Chapter 11 (New Testament)
Please read and meditate on this entire chapter!

CHAPTER FIVE

CHANGE/GROWTH IS A MYSTERY!

—〰—

M y mother gave me a brief smile as she was carted off to the operating room at Mount Sinai Hospital in upper Manhattan. It was early in the morning and I nervously clutched a Bible as the nurses pushed her down the hallway on a stretcher into a big room with glass doors. I could only think of the time that had passed and the many battles my mother faced over the past year and a half after being diagnosed with a rare form of cancer that was slowly taking her life. The doctors said that she might not make it out of the operating room this time around.

I remember sneaking up on her in a hospital room at Mary Immaculate Hospital in Queens before she was diagnosed with the disease. Enola Laws Phillips was lying in a bed staring straight up at the ceiling with her fingertips pressed together. I just looked at her for a moment, wondering what must have been going through her mind. She did not seem at all worried, but after two major strokes that could have killed her or left her crippled earlier in life, she now faced a new challenge at the age of 78. Doctors could not seem to determine what was causing two bulges in the veins of her neck. After a few moments studying my mother, I leaped into the room and startled her. Knowing my nature of being a prankster, my mother laughed and we talked like we always did. I can't remember the conversation at the time. The thing is we talked about so many things over the years. She was truly my best friend and not a day would go by that we didn't talk about something! Our conversations were always lengthy, we just never seemed to run out of things to talk about. From politics to religion, or just clowning around, I always hung up the phone feeling good that I made contact with mom. You see, she was a source of comfort and seemed to know exactly what to do if she sensed I needed help or guidance. I can remember getting an article in the mail about some subject we talked about—or more importantly a scripture from the bible with a note attached to it after telling her about some trouble or challenge I was facing at the time.

Mom had lost a lot of weight after months of being sick. This form of cancer was robbing her of oxygen and the slow growing tumors were squeezing her lungs shut. It seemed like a part of me was dying right along with her as I watched her go through numerous procedures to keep her alive and functioning. As she lost weight, so did I. While the cancer slowly advanced on her body, I was involved in the midst of another battle. That being the much anticipated separation from my wife Barbara. At this point, Barbara had taken a three month singing job overseas in Dubai. While we were separated, we always maintained contact. Now she was gone, mom was sick and felt I was facing the world alone. The prospect of mom not being around….She was my only source of strength. Now I was in the unusual position of trying to comfort her.

As the doctors performed delicate surgery, I sat inside a waiting room and read the entire book of Isaiah. This prophet was her favorite and she would always send me a scripture or two from this book when she felt I needed strength. What better book to read, I thought to myself—so I did. After a few hours, mom emerged on the stretcher from the operating room and I was there to greet her. She came out with a smile and gave me the thumbs up sign. "It's not as bad as it looks Julian" she said as they wheeled her off to her room. Mom looked like she had gone through hell and I couldn't help but cry as I followed her on the stretcher.

At this point, my life had taken a turn for the worse. A dying mom and a painful separation. What next? When would there be a change for the better? I spent hours praying for change. Praying that God would find a miracle cure for my mother and resolve this separation from Barbara. A few months earlier, I got saved at the Christian Life Center in Brooklyn. Armed with this new hope and faith being a born-again Christian, life surely would take a turn for the better! Over the next few months I went on a trek with one of my church buddies. He made it a habit of traveling to various churches, listening to different pastors preach the Gospel and invited me to tag along. A number of these churches were small storefront establishments in Brooklyn. A few were quite 'different' from my usual experiences visiting 'houses of the Lord'. In one place, I was told to turn around seven times in a circle and pray for a cure for my mother. It all sounded so crazy, but at this point I was desperate and tried almost anything to change life as it presented itself to me at the time. Nothing seemed to work. Mom's condition continued to get worse and I started to sink into a depression.

One day after a Sunday service, I decided to seek comfort from Pastor Bernard about how God might work in my life and change things for the better."Your mother is going to die Julian and this will happen so you will be able grow and develop". What?! Did pastor say what I thought he said? It was so opposite from what I expected to hear from him. Not wanting to hear anything else, I changed the subject and went home after service, but what he said lingered in my mind the rest of that day—and long after my mother passed.

It was Mother's Day almost a year after mom died and I sat outside on a wooden bench at my mother-in-law's house. There was good news in that Barbara and I were in a period of reconciliation but the pain of mom's passing remained strong in my mind. As you can probably imagine, the memories started to come on that warm sunny spring day—and so did the tears. I must have cried nearly a half-hour on that bench. After months of prayer and counsel, it seemed God was starting to reunite me with my wife. However, mom, my heart and soul was gone. How could this mighty prayer go unanswered, I thought? Could it be that God does not fulfill all the requests his children make? Needless to say I had considerable doubt about prayer and it's effectiveness at this time in my life.

Several months had passed and Barbara and I were back together. While life was getting good, there were a few major rough spots. Barbara's father passed away from a short battle with cancer. He was the family rock and the loss was devastating. It was a major loss for me as well, because all throughout our separation, her father and I remained good friends and often hung out together.

Barbara and I took a stroll one late afternoon along the dock in town and watched the sun set over Manhasset Bay. We took stock of our lives and where God had taken us. We talked about the pain of separation and the death of her father and my mother, wishing that God could have spared their lives to witness both our reunion and new home we shared on Long Island. Why couldn't they be here to enjoy this, I wondered? It was then that the words of pastor Bernard came exploding back into my head about death and development. While it was painful—and I still wish my mother was here, I could see now that my total dependency for most everything revolved around my mother. In a sense I was not maturing as a man as long as mom was there to make things right. I could not see it at the time, but after mom's death, I started to grow-up—mature. My 'crutch' was taken away. The process of change could be seen by a lot of people, especially Barbara who now witnessed a man whose character was strengthened through trial and challenge. While I miss mom, I thanked God for the long life he had given her as well as the great times we shared. I still wish both she and my father-in-law were here but I could see how God used suffering and death to help transform a life in need. *My life*. The question I still often think about is could there have been a better way? I guess change and growth is a mystery at times.

CHANGE/GROWTH

When we look back at history, the wars, the famines, the slaughters, the sickness, the disease, the illnesses of man and at the same time the advancement, the progress and the question is has man changed? Has humanity changed? I have to agree with someone that I admire so much—don't agree fully with everything Will Durant made a comment about human history. He said that humans have changed their behavior through laws, policies, procedure, but human nature has remained the same. Now that's interesting, because there's an essence of who we are as humans and in our faith tradition as Christians, we know that the human condition presently is in alienation from God and because of that alienation, man behaves contrary to his own health, to his own progress and to the progress of his community. And unless he disciplines himself, that human nature will run wild and rampant—destroy him and destroy his society. So we've learned how to discipline our behavior individually and corporately, but man is still by nature, who he has been since the fall of Adam.

Are you looking for the change that frees you from the struggle that is making you who you are? Because if that is the change you are looking for—without that struggle you would not grow. There is resistance to growth. Everything in this universe as it is right now is designed to grow and to mature. But we are also in a state of resistance to that growth and to that maturity.

We live in parallel worlds, the spiritual and the natural and quite often the natural things are obvious to us but we don't see the spiritual parallels so the spiritual seems so removed. If you decide to go into bodybuilding, they'll tell you that you need to consistently follow a certain regimen for 6 months before you will see any noticable change. Yet we want to see change instantly within the first few attempts of anything. Change takes time, it takes discipline, it takes consistency and commitment to change.

Dr. A.R. Bernard

Some scriptures for you to consider while in your season of change. God bless.

Proverbs Chapter 21 verse 1
The king's heart is in the hands of the Lord; he directs it like a watercourse wherever he pleases. NIV (Old Testament)

Proverbs Chapter 3 verse 25
Have no fear of sudden disaster or of the ruin that overtakes the wicked, for the Lord will be your confidence and will keep your foot from being snared. NIV (Old Testament)

Proverbs Chapter 4 verses 11-13
I guide you in the way of wisdom and lead you along straight paths. When you walk, your steps will not be hampered; when you run, you will not stumble. Hold on to instruction; do not let it go; guard it well, for it is your life. NIV (Old Testament)

Jeremiah Chapter 10 verses 23-24
I know, O lord, that a man's life is not his own; it is not for man to direct his steps, Correct me Lord, but only with justice..... NIV (Old Testament)

2 Thessalonians Chapter 3 verse 5
*May the Lord direct your hearts into God's love...*NIV (Old Testament)

CHAPTER SIX

STAND!

—⚍—

W e had a pretty big clothing closet at our first home on Long Island—but it wasn't big enough for Barbara not to hear my sniveling and short sobs several feet from where she was standing. Turning around inside the closet, she saw the tears streaming down my face. "What in the world is wrong with you?" she asked with a puzzled and somewhat startled look on her face. "I don't know if I can do this job," I said to her. "It's not what I thought it was going to be. I've never done anything like this before!"

I was referring to the world of cable network news. A 24 hour non-stop grind of events around the globe happening live and uncensored. A fast paced world of news and information. Anchors, reporters, producers, bookers and writers and assistants scurrying to deliver this news to eager viewers huddled around TV screens inside homes, hotels, on planes and remote outposts near the battlefields in Iraq and Afghanistan. Fox News Channel, the number one cable news network seen in 87 countries and 103 million households worldwide—and they had just hired little ol' me as a weekend anchor/reporter!

"What God has for you is yours alone!" I shouted to 15 thousand members of the Christian Cultural Center in Brooklyn as some stood while others sat and applauded. It was a great day and pastor had me share my testimony with the congregants about this new job. After all the praying and waiting for something *big* to happen in my career, the move from local reporter to network cable news anchor was indeed a very big deal. Even some folks at the old station scratched their heads and wondered how I was able to pull this one off! After all I didn't have an agent representing me. I fired the one I had years before. Most people could not or would not acknowledge or comprehend what I had been saying for a few years now that I had *another* agent representing me. Remember the chapter on faith? Well this of course was the culmination of that faith and I knew and still know to this day that only God could have paved the way for such a career leap!

"Don't give up!" I shouted with more confidence the longer I spoke. "Use me as just another example of God's power in your lives. There is something greater out there for you!" My voice broke several times throughout the testimony and I almost started to cry tears of joy. After the church service, I thought to myself how embarrassing it all was, but it was real and a lot of folk said they heard a message they could sink their teeth into.

The next day I entered the halls of Fox News. An anchor position was just the thing I was looking for. A chance to get off the streets and sit back and read the news, I said to myself. What could be easier? After all I'd been a substitute anchor before at the local station. It was relatively easy. Almost everything was handed to you. Maybe you edited some scripts an hour or so before the news cast, but that was it besides the make-up. Just look good and go out there on the set and make the viewers *think* you're actually interested in the stuff you're telling them, I would say to myself. I heard through the grapevine, network anchoring was about the same, so I figured this was going to be a cakewalk— Julian has finally made the big-time!

Fox News Channel was riding high for a few years now. CNN, the recognized cable news giant for years was a distant second place in the ratings and Fox CEO Roger Ailes was the brainchild behind all the success. This is truly a modern day David and Goliath story. Ailes took this upstart network with few resources at the time and defied the odds against a seemingly unbeatable foe. Who would have thunk it?! Now Ailes is somewhat of a charismatic figure. I'd say a genius at being able to lead and influence people. Before I interviewed with him, I read his book *"You are the Message"* a great read on his philosophy of the news biz and life in general. I actually was impressed with his take on management and leadership so I was eager to become a part of the Fox team. Ailes wanted to beef-up the weekend ratings and I was proud to be a part of that effort. My first assignment was weekend anchor for Fox News Live.

"You'll have about 6 guests to interview for the hour and a half you are on the air" said one of the producers assigned to the 2 o'clock show. Patti Anne Brown will be your co-anchor when you start after this week's orientation period. "We are focusing on terror as you may know and we will probably have someone from the Department of Defense and the Department of State for you to interview". "Do we have any information on these people?" I asked somewhat nervously. "Oh yes, you'll be provided with a lot of back-ground information, plus some suggested questions." Oh, ok, I said somewhat relieved. In the background, the moni-tors were on the live telecast taking place inside Studio B upstairs. "This is a Fox News Alert! The President is about to make remarks at a luncheon honoring…." I heard about three more of these alerts on other subjects within 15 minutes of the first alert. All were preceded by this weird gong. The words then seemed to flow with relative ease from the mouths of the anchors who delivered the alerts. Then it was back to the interview they were involved in at the time, or the report they were giving. "Tell me about these alerts," I asked. "Are they scripted and do they come up often during any given show?" "Well that depends on the day," the producer explained. "Some days there is a lot of breaking news and it comes in hot and heavy. And by the way, most are not scripted. You'll have a laptop computer at the anchor desk. We'll tell you where to look for the information. Sometimes there may be a lot—other times you might have a sentence or two for background. Then there are other times we'll just tell you what we know and you have to go with it."

Sheer terror started to take control! Partially unscripted news cast? Alerts aided in part by a laptop computer and producers barking out information in your ear sometimes seconds before you are supposed to make sense of it on the air? What about these interviews? I hosted three talk shows in my career, but they were taped and all on local issues. Things I was very familiar with. The worse part was I hated computers. Never worked a laptop in my life and here I am faced with all of this with one week before show time! What did I get myself into? I had just given this bold testimony before 15 thousand Christians and within less that a week,

I'd certainly face total humiliation on international television! Was this a God ordained mission as I so boldly testified at last Sunday's service or did I finally bite off more than I could chew?

Barbara did not say much to me in that closet other than she was certain things would be alright. That was not nearly enough to comfort me so I once again called on pastor Bernard for advice—and once again hearing a message that should have been directed to the man on the moon! "Don't worry Julian; God is just stretching you," is all he would say. I should have known by this time that Pastor Bernard was not going to tell me anything that would provide great relief. Conversely, he delivered a message of faith and trust.

Could faith and trust get me past the huge hurdle of fear and worry? I had huge doubts. What immediately came to mind was the story about the prophet Elijah in the Old Testament and how after a great victory over 500 fake prophets—he was reduced to running for his life into the hills from Jezebel the witch! I certainly felt like Elijah back then.

What did I have to go on? Well that week I went to church and pastor made arrangements for me to take one of the church laptops into my office to use for practice—as well as attend to some church business. Before leaving I went to the church bookstore to find something suitable for the office. I picked up this framed scripture:

"For I know the plans I have for you," **declares the Lord.** *"Plans to prosper you and not to harm you, plans to give you hope and a future."*

Jeremiah 29:11 NIV

I meditated on that for the week to prepare myself for Saturday's debut.

In the meantime, a few of the security guards in the building would always greet me with enthusiasm. A couple would always say with a smile "you're the first one." First what?! I found out they meant I was the first black male anchor they had seen at Fox and it was a sense of pride for them to see me there. One more burden to bear I thought.

Patti Anne Browne greeted me on the set. She was well established at Fox and a seasoned professional. On top of that she had a calm spirit and made me feel at ease. After I logged in, we chatted for a bit during a commercial break and then within seconds it was show time. "I'd like to take this opportunity to welcome Julian Phillips to the Fox Family. He is a new anchor here." "Thank you Patti Ann, it's glad to be here."—*It's* glad to be here, I said to myself? How about I'm glad to be here you idiot! The next 20 minutes was all downhill. The make-up artist must have ventured on the set at least a dozen times to wipe the sweat off my face. The debut could not have been worse in my mind and I left the set after the show a little more than dejected. However, I knew there was no turning back. I figured I had done all the preparing I could do. I got books on politics and international conflict. One of the producers, Mykel McCarthy came up to my office on a regular basis and we performed "mock alerts" on my laptop. The only thing I could do now was **stand.**

Less than two months later I was a regular fill-in for John Scott. Scott anchored the 9 am show and that was considered an important show to start off the news day after the Fox & Friends morning show, so I figured I'd made some prog-ress. I still felt uncomfortable with the alerts—and had avoided having to do many until Thanksgiving Day. Jennifer Starobin was the regular producer for the 9 o'clock hour and she loved working with me. She was very demanding in that she moved around her anchors on the set like a chess pieces. You opened the show standing up in front of camera one, then you anchored a bit from the news desk .The next thing you know you are away from the laptop and anchoring from the War Desk. Was this anchoring or news aerobics? Anyway, we all thought it would be a light news day until word came in literally seconds before the newscast of a bomb blast inside a Jewish resort in Africa—and shortly after that a shoulder-fired missile fired at a chartered jet headed back to Israel! The next hour and a half was completely crazy. New information was coming in almost every minute. Alerts galore and Starobin plus other producers were in my ear the entire time with more information. Phoners with terror experts were being arranged. In the middle of all of this, there's this guy, Julian Phillips charged with the task of making sense of this for our viewers!

At the end of the show, Jennifer came and gave me a hug for a job well done and I heard from a few other people on the staff as well. I went back up to my office to try to take it all in. Had I finally *arrived?* Well I'm not convinced anyone actually makes it to that point. I knew after getting this job there was no looking back. I smiled to myself after pastor's comments about God stretching me came back into my mind. I also knew, even if pride was at the core of it all, I was going to make a **stand.** Despite what it looked like, I would move forward in this job and let the chips fall where they may. After a few minutes thinking over the last two hours I glanced over at the framed scripture I purchased from the church bookstore.

STANDING

When the wind is blowing, you are not standing idle—you're standing in a position of resistance! That wind is pushing to send you backward, but you're making sure that having done all that you could to move forward, you've reached a point that you cannot go forward—standing is refusing to go backwards! It's refusing to lose the ground that you've gained, the time, effort, the price that you've paid to get you to that point where you are standing. Standing is a refusal to let all of that be in vain! That is why the armor of God protects the entire front, not our back! The breastplate of righteousness, the shield of faith, the sword of the spirit, the helmet of salvation, everything that's for forward movement, not backward movement!

Dr. A.R. Bernard

Some scriptures to help you stand.

Isaiah Chapter 43 Verses 1-3
*…"Fear not, for I have redeemed you; I have summoned you by name; you are mine. When you pass through the waters, I will be with you; and when you pass through the rivers, they will not sweep over you. When you walk through the fire, you will not be burned; the flames will not set you ablaze. For I am the Lord, your God, the Holy One of Israel, your Savior ;…*NIV (Old Testament)

Psalm 37 verse 25
"I was young and now I am old, yet I have never seen the righteous forsaken or their children begging bread." NIV (Old Testament)

Psalm 46 verses 1-2
*"God is our refuge and strength, an ever-present help in trouble. Therefore we will not fear…"*NIV (Old Testament)

James 4 verse 7
"...Resist the devil, and he will flee from you." NIV (New Testament)

Exodus 14 verse 13
*"...Do not be afraid. Stand firm and you will see the deliverance the Lord will bring you today..."*NIV (Old Testament)

CHAPTER SEVEN

THEY WILL SOAR ON WINGS LIKE EAGLES!

—⚬—

Summer was fast approaching and the track season thankfully started to wind down. While I was good at track, I hated the competition of one-on-one events. I preferred team sports where it usually took more than one person to decide the outcome. I had quit the boy's varsity basketball team at Martin Van Buren High School in Queens Village earlier in the year and that is way too long of a story to get into now, but I did join a local basketball league in the neighborhood which took up a lot of my spare time. Besides the play, it gave me an excuse to avoid track meets when I could. Track coach Al Capelli was very demanding and we had a top rated track team. In fact, on many occasions we were rated in the top ten in the city. Our mile relay team was very well respected and I would occasionally fill in when needed to run the second or third leg. Now not all the members of the team were excited about my appearances. I never went to many practices and oftentimes some of my friends on the team as well as coach Capelli would routinely track me down between classes and ask if I could participate in a meet. "Your parents are going to think this is an easy sport!" Cappelli shouted to me with disgust written all over his face after a meet on Randalls Island. We'd just won the mile relay in a sectional and it just so happened I filled in that day. I usually won some sort of medal when I ran. I was gifted but the reason why I didn't like to participate in practice or meets was once again, not arrogance—but **fear.** Fear was something that plagued me most of my life. I'm not sure why. I can't pin it all on my father and his negativity although I'm sure some of that came into play. Despite all the medals, I hated one-on-one competition—even when it came to relay races.

Near the end of the school year, the track team focused on the Northeast Queens Championships. This was far from the biggest meet of the year, but it gave bragging rights to the school that could claim to be the best in northeast Queens.

Somehow Capelli was able to get me to run the third leg in the mile relay event. Four guys running 440 yards flat out. Some say it is the hardest race in track. I'm no expert, but I'll say it's a very tough race!

About a month before the meet, the local basketball league was winding down. We had just finished practice when one of my team mates approached me. "I heard you're running the third leg in the North East Queens Championships," Phil said with a scowl on his face. "I'm gonna kick you're a__, I'll smoke you!" Phil ran track for rival Francis Lewis high school. He was about 6 feet 6, had muscles growing out of his ears and was blacker than asphalt. To say he was intimidating was putting it mildly. Now I mentioned earlier, fear was a major factor as to why I avoided track meets like the plague, and it started to consume me. I never recalled seeing him run and I don't think he ever witnessed me in a race. I also mentioned earlier, Martin Van Buren had a reputation for fielding one of the best mile relay teams in the city. The problem was I never ran with any frequency on that team. Perhaps Phil knew that, perhaps he didn't, but why was he so confident he could devour me on the track, I'll never know. Of course I gave it more thought that I should have, but despite my talent and abilities I felt like the cowardly lion standing before the Wizard of Oz in his presence!

For the better part of a month, Phil would badger me in basketball practice about the upcoming meet. He was certainly a good trash talker—and pretty convincing to boot. I guess a lot of it had to do with his outward appearance.

After weeks of hearing Phil talk trash, the meet was finally upon us. The mile relay was the marquee event and needless to say the wait until the end of the meet for this show down of sorts was eating at what was left of my already frayed nerves. Phil had already shredded his warm-ups. With his ego the size of the Grand Canyon, he was more than eager to show off his muscles to the girls in the crowd.

We were favored to win and my teammates were not concerned about Francis Lewis or Phil for that matter—but something happened on the second leg of the relay to our runner. Somehow he either slipped or was having a bad day—it's been too many years to remember, but we wound up behind Francis Lewis coming into the last turn before the hand-off to the third leg! Now I'm standing there next to Phil, who was also running the third leg like me, witnessing this unfold and he could not contain himself. "You don't stand a chance now. We've got this race, chump!"

The second runner for Francis Lewis came in at least twenty yards or so before my guy handed me the baton. I could see Phil's big feet kick-up dust going down the track as I waited for what seemed like an eternity for my guy to hand me the baton. I don't know why, but I didn't feel any fear at that moment, I just wanted the baton. After the handoff I sprinted towards the turn. It seemed like only an instant, but I must have made up about ten yards on Phil near the end of the first turn. I could vaguely hear the screams from the crowd and my confidence kicked-in. By the middle of the back stretch I completely closed the gap. Phil and I were neck and neck. I took one glance over at Phil then took off around the last turn. By the time I reached my anchor to finish the race I put a ten yard gap between me and him. A ten yard gap, man! Now you gotta understand his twenty yard lead is something that is almost impossible to overcome for a *quality* runner. Looking back on things now, Phil had less quality in his ability. He could not back up his entire month of trash talking.

I'm not proud to say that after the race I had to do a little trash talking of my own. Phil got more than an earful and I'm sure he was embarrassed. For me, it still ranks as one of the best moments of my life. What a thrill! Someone managed to capture me making the last turn on a Polaroid camera. After all these years, I've lost track of that snapshot, but I believe it may be in my sisters' attic with a lot of memories collecting dust from the old neighborhood. I think I'll try to dig it up.

The thing here is that I resisted the temptation of falling victim to all the trash talking before the event. I patiently waited for the race and let my abilities do the talking for me on the field. That does not mean I was not scared. I was — but I prepared for it in advance, hoping that the work I put in would produce the victory. Boy did I soar that day. I felt like the nickname I gave myself when I first started running track. 'Winged Soul."

"...but those who hope in the Lord will renew their strength. They will soar on wings like eagles; they will run and not grow weary, they will walk and not be faint." NIV

Isaiah 40:31

TRUE VICTORY

True victory is not the victory that feeds the ego—but is the victory that strengthens the spirit and becomes fuel to overcome obstacles in the future. When David faced Goliath what strengthened him was remembering God's strength in his life when he faced the bear, when he faced the lion. He saw Goliath not as something to feed his ego, but a cause. He saw it as something that defied all that he believed and stood for. This uncircumcised Philistine (Goliath) stood defying God Himself and David felt in his spirit, the strength that he gathered from his past experiences, his past victories and he said 'is there not a cause' and he took up that cause, fueled by those smaller victories and he faced this giant. That is true victory. But it (victory) doesn't stroke the ego when we say look at me, but it strengthens us so deeply that it prepares us for the greater challenges and obstacles in the future.

Dr. A.R. Bernard

****

I hope and pray that the stories presented in this book benefit those who read them. Life can indeed be difficult and we all need pearls of wisdom dropped in our lives to help us along this journey. The other day a friend mentioned that she wanted to try cross-country skiing because she thought it would be much easier than trying her hand at downhill skiing, which to her seemed much more difficult and dangerous. "Sooner or later you will run out of a flat surface and you're gonna have to deal with some hills and valleys," I told her. Isn't that the same in life? There will be some hills and some valleys. Sometimes mountains thrown in the mix too! Are you equipped to deal with them? What **power** do you possess? The scriptures have been tested over thousands of years. God's Word has proved to be worthy, of great value to those who read and believe. Give them a try. Recite them. Meditate on them. I have given just a few throughout this book that have been a great help to me. I pray these will inspire you to search the Bible for many more scriptures to strengthen you in times of need. I pray your journey or the one for the person to whom you may present this book will be blessed and empowered for success, abundance and peace!

In His service,

Julian Phillips

LaVergne, TN USA
21 September 2010
197864LV00003B/134/P